POP
ROCK

MELODY LINE, CHORDS AND LYRICS
FOR KEYBOARD • GUITAR • VOCAL

HAL•LEONARD®

ISBN 0-634-04065-0

Printed in Canada

HAL•LEONARD®
CORPORATION
7777 W. BLUEMOUND RD. P.O. BOX 13819 MILWAUKEE, WI 53213

Visit Hal Leonard Online at
www.halleonard.com

Welcome to the PAPERBACK SONGS SERIES.

Do you play piano, guitar, electronic keyboard, sing or play any instrument for that matter? If so, this handy "pocket tune" book is for you.

The concise, one-line music notation consists of:

MELODY, LYRICS & CHORD SYMBOLS

Whether strumming the chords on guitar, "faking" an arrangement on piano/keyboard or singing the lyrics, these fake book style arrangements can be enjoyed at any experience level – hobbyist to professional.

The musical skills necessary to successfully use this book are minimal. If you play guitar and need some help with chords, a basic chord chart is included at the back of the book.

While playing and singing is the first thing that comes to mind when using this book, it can also serve as a compact, comprehensive reference guide.

However you choose to use this PAPERBACK SONGS SERIES book, by all means have fun!

CONTENTS

(contents continued)

8

ALL YOU NEED IS LOVE

Words and Music by JOHN LENNON
and PAUL McCARTNEY

10

All You Need Is Love. __

All You Need Is Love. __ Love __

Love is all __ you need.

D.S. al Coda

CODA

All You Need Is Love __

__ (All to-geth-er now) __ All You Need Is Love __

__ (Ev - 'ry - bod - y) All You Need Is Love __

__ Love __ Love is all __ you need.

Repeat and Fade

Love is all _____ you need.
Love is all __ you need.
Love is all __

ANGEL

Words and Music by
SARAH McLACHLAN

12

14

15

ANOTHER DAY
IN PARADISE

Words and Music by
PHIL COLLINS

She calls out __ to the man __ on the street, __
He walks on, __   does-n't look back, __
She calls out __ to the man __ on the street. __
You can tell __ from the lines __ on her face, __

"Sir __ can you help __ me?"
He pre - tends __ he can't hear __ her.
He can see __ she's been cry - ing.
you can see __ that she's been __ there.

"It's cold __ and I've no - where to sleep. __
Starts to whis - tle as he cross-es the street, __
She's got blis - ters on the souls of her feet. __
Prob - a - bly been moved on from ev - er - y place, __

Is there some - where _ you can tell __ me?"
seems em - bar - rassed to be
She can't walk, __ but she's try -
'cos she did - n't fit in __

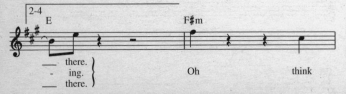

__ there.
- ing.
__ there.

Oh   think

17

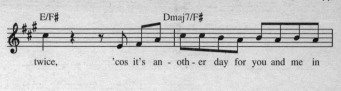

twice, 'cos it's an-oth-er day for you and me in

par - a - dise. ___ Oh think

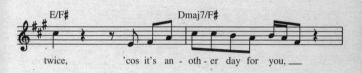

twice, 'cos it's an-oth-er day for you, ___

you and me in par - a - dise. ___ (Instrumental)

Think a-bout ___ it. (Instrumental)

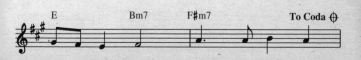

18

BEST OF MY LOVE

Words and Music by JOHN DAVID SOUTHER,
DON HENLEY and GLENN FREY

Moderately slow

Ev - er - y night _ I'm ly - in' in bed, ___
Beau - ti - ful fac - es and loud emp - ty plac - es, _

hold - in' you close _ in my dreams; _
look at the way that we live; ___

think - in' a - bout _ all the things that we _ said _ and
wast - in' our time _ on cheap talk and wine

com - in' a - part ___ at the seams. _
left us so _ lit - tle to give. _

We try to talk it o - ver but the
That same old crowd was like a cold dark cloud that

words come out _ too _ rough; _ I
we could nev - er rise a - bove; _ but

know you were try - in' to give me the best _ of your _
here in my heart ___ I give you the best _ of my _

love.

love.
Oh, _____

_____ sweet dar - lin',
you get the best of my

love, ___
oh, _____
sweet dar - lin',

you get the best of my ___ love.
I'm go-in'

back in time ___ and it's a sweet _____ dream; ___

it was a qui - et night ___ and I would

be all ___ right if I could go _____ on sleep - ing. But

ev - 'ry morn - in' I wake up and wor - ry _____

Dm7

what's gon - na hap - pen to - day. ____

C

You see it your _ way and I see it mine, _ but we

Dm7

both see it slip - pin' a - way. ____

Em7   Dm7

You know we al - ways had each oth - er, ba - by,

Em7   Dm7   G7

I guess that was-n't e - nough; ____ oh, ____ but

C   Dm7

here in my heart _ I give you the best _ of my _

C   G7   C

love.   Oh, ____   sweet dar -

Repeat and Fade

Dm7   Dm7/G

- lin',   you get the best of my love. _   Oh, ____

BE-BOP-A-LULA

Words and Music by TEX DAVIS
and GENE VINCENT

Moderately slow Rock

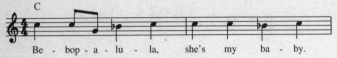

Be - bop - a - lu - la, she's my ba - by.

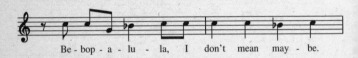

Be - bop - a - lu - la, I don't mean may - be.

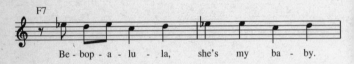

Be - bop - a - lu - la, she's my ba - by.

Be - bop - a - lu - la, I don't mean may - be.

Be - bop - a - lu - la, she's my ba - by

doll, my ba - by doll, my ba - by doll.

BLUE SUEDE SHOES

Words and Music by
CARL LEE PERKINS

Bright tempo (not too fast)

Well, it's one for the mon - ey, two for the show, three to get read - y, now go, cat, go. But don't you step on my Blue Suede Shoes. You can do an - y - thing but lay off of my Blue Suede Shoes. Well, you can knock me down, step on my face, burn my house, steal my car,

25

CALIFORNIA GIRLS

Words and Music by BRIAN WILSON
and MIKE LOVE

Moderate Shuffle Rock

Well, east coast girls are hip; I really
west coast has the sun-shine and the

dig those styles they wear. ___ And the
girls all get so tan. ___ I dig a

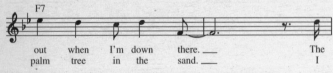

south-ern girls ___ with ___ the way they talk, ___ they knock me
French bi-ki-ni on Ha-wai-ian is-lands, dolls by a

out when I'm down there. ___ The
palm tree in the sand. ___ I

mid-west farm-er's daugh-ters real-ly make you feel al-
been all a-round this great big world, and I've seen all kinds of

right, ___ and ___ north-ern girls ___ with ___ the
girls, ___ but I could-n't wait ___ to ___ get

way they kiss ___ they keep their boy-friends warm at night. ___
back in the states ___ back to the cut-est girls in the world.

Bb

I wish they all could be ___

Cm7   **Ab**

___ Cal - i - for - nia, I wish they all could be ___

Bbm   **Gb**

___ Cal - i - for - nia, I wish they all could be ___

Abm |1 **Bb**

___ Cal - i - for - nia girls. ___

|2 **Bb**

___ The girls. ___

N.C.

(Instrumental)   I

Bb

wish they all could be ___ Cal - i - for - nia, I

Eb   **Repeat and Fade**

wish they all could be ___ Cal - i - for - nia, I

CENTERFOLD

Words and Music by
SETH JUSTMAN

nev - er cause ____ me pain. The
take 'em off ____ in pri - vate. A

years go by, I'm look-in' through a girl-ie mag - a - zine, and
part of me has just been ripped, the pag-es from my mind are stripped.

there's my home - room an - gel on the
Ah no! I can't de - ny it.

pag - es in be - tween.
Oh yeah, I guess I got-ta buy it. } My

blood runs cold; _ my mem-o - ry ____ has just been sold. My

an - gel is the cen - ter - fold.

An - gel is the cen - ter - fold. My

blood runs cold; _ my mem-o - ry ____ has just been sold.

To Coda ⊕

(Instrumental) An - gel in the cen-ter-fold.

31

COME SAIL AWAY

Words and Music by
DENNIS DeYOUNG

Moderately slow

I'm sail - ing _____ a - way.
I've got to _____ be free,

Set an o - pen course for the vir - gin sea. Cause
free to face the life that's a - head of me.

On board I'm the cap-tain, _____ so climb a - board.

We'll search for to-mor-row _____ on ev - 'ry shore, _____ and I'll

try, oh Lord, _____ I'll try

to car - ry on.

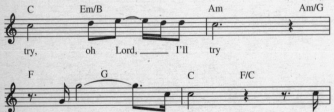

gath - er - ing _____ of an - gels _____ ap -
thought that they _____ were an - gels _____ but

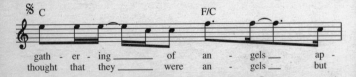

CRIMSON AND CLOVER

Words and Music by TOMMY JAMES
and PETER LUCIA

Moderately slow

Oh, now, I don't hard - ly know

— her, — but, I think I could love

— her, — crim - son and clo -

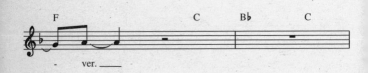

- ver. ____

I wish she'd come walk - ing o -
Yes, my, my, such a sweet

- ver. ___   I'm wait-ing to show ___

___ thing. _   I want to do ev - er - y -

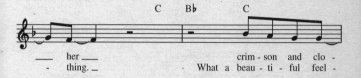

___ her ___   crim - son and clo -

- thing. _   What a beau - ti - ful feel -

- ver, ___   o - ver and o -

- ing. ___   Crim - son and clo -

To Coda ⊕

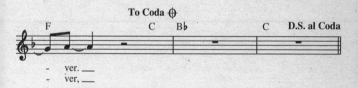

- ver. ___

- ver, ___

CODA

⊕

o - ver and o - ver. ___

Repeat and Fade

Crim - son and clo - ver,   o - ver and o - ver.

CRYING

Words and Music by ROY ORBISON
and JOE MELSON

Moderately slow, with feeling

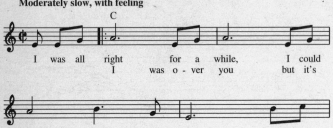

I was all right for a while, I could
I was o - ver you but it's

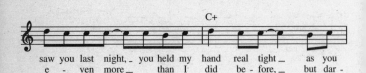

smile for a while. But I
true so _____ true I love you

saw you last night, _ you held my hand real tight _ as you
e - ven more _ than I did be - fore, _ but dar -

stopped to say "Hel - lo." Oh, you
ling, what can I do? For you

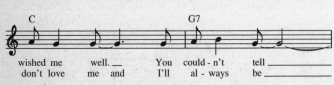

wished me well. _ You could - n't tell _____
don't love me and I'll al - ways be _____

_____ that I'd been cry - ing o - ver you

DO THAT TO ME
ONE MORE TIME

Words and Music by
TONI TENNILLE

DON'T BE CRUEL
(To a Heart That's True)

Words and Music by OTIS BLACKWELL
and ELVIS PRESLEY

Medium bright (with a beat)

You know I can be found sitting home all a-lone if you can't come a-round, at least, please tel-e-phone. Don't Be Cruel to a heart that's true.

Baby, if I made you mad for some-thing I might have said please let's for-get the past the future looks bright a-head. Don't Be Cruel to a heart that's true. I don't want no oth-er love, Ba-by, it's just

G7   C

you   I'm   think-ing   of. ____

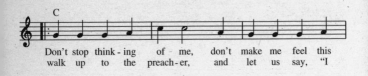

C

Don't stop think-ing   of   me,   don't make me feel this
walk   up   to   the   preach-er,   and   let   us   say, "I

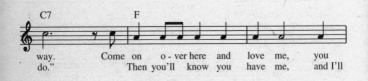

C7   F

way.   Come on   o - ver here   and   love me,   you
do."   Then you'll   know   you   have me,   and I'll

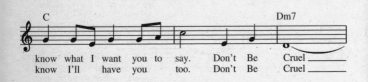

C   Dm7

know what I want you to say. Don't Be   Cruel ____
know I'll   have   you   too.   Don't Be   Cruel ____

G7   C

____ to   a heart that's   true. ____   Why
____ to   a heart that's   true. ____   I don't

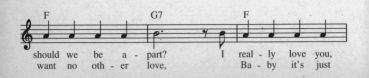

F   G7   F

should we   be   a - part?   I   real - ly   love you,
want no   oth - er   love,   Ba - by   it's   just

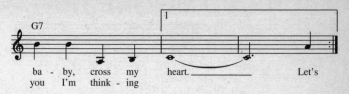

ba - by, cross my heart. _____ Let's
you I'm think - ing

of. _____ Don't Be Cruel _____

___ to a heart that's true. _____ Don't Be

Cruel _____ to a heart that's true. _____

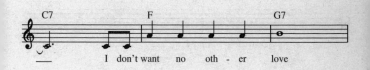

___ I don't want no oth - er love

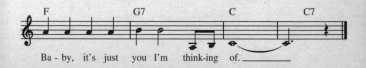

Ba - by, it's just you I'm think-ing of. _____

DON'T DO ME LIKE THAT

Words and Music by
TOM PETTY

Moderately

(1.) I was talk-in' with a friend of mine,_
(2., D.C.) Lis-ten, hon-ey, can't you see?_

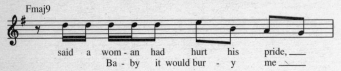

said a wom-an had hurt his pride,____
Ba-by it would bur-y me_____

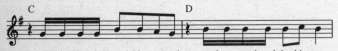

told him that she loved him so and turned a-round and let him go.
if you were in the pub-lic eye,_ giv-in' some-one else a try.

Then he said, "You bet-ter watch your step
And you know you bet-ter watch your step

or you're gon-na get hurt your-self._ Some-one's gon-na tell you lies,

cut you down to size." Don't do me like that. Don't do me like that.

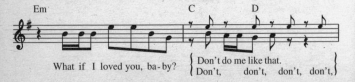

What if I loved you, ba-by? Don't do me like that.
Don't, don't, don't, don't,

43

G   Fmaj9   **To Coda** ⊕

Don't do me like that.   Don't do me like that.

1 Em   C   D

Some-day I might need you, ba - by.   Don't do me like that.

2 Em   C   D

What if I need you, ba-by?   Don't do me like that,   'cause

G7   C7

some-where deep, down in - side, _ some-one is say - in', "Love_

G7   C7

_ does - n't last _ that _ long."_

G7   C7

I've had this feel-in' in - side _ night out and day _ in,   and

Cm   D   **D.C. al Coda**

ba-by I can't take _ it no more. _

CODA   **D.S. and Fade**
⊕ Em   C   D **(Vocal ad lib.)**

I just might_need you, hon - ey.   Don't do me like that.

DREAM ON

Words and Music by
STEVEN TYLER

45

47

DUST IN THE WIND

Words and Music by
KERRY LIVGREN

49

ELVIRA

Words and Music by
DALLAS FRAZIER

Moderate Country beat

El - vi - ra, El - vi - ra,

my heart's on fi - re for El -

vi - ra. Eyes that look like
night I'm gon - na

heav - en. Lips like cher - ry wine. That
meet her at the Hun - gry House Ca - fe, and

girl can sho' nuff make my lit - tle light
I'm gon - na give her all the love I

shine. _____
can. _____

I get a fun - ny
She's gon - na jump and

feel - ing up and down my spine,
hol - ler, 'cause I saved up my last two dol - lar, and

EVERY BREATH YOU TAKE

Written and Composed by
STING

54

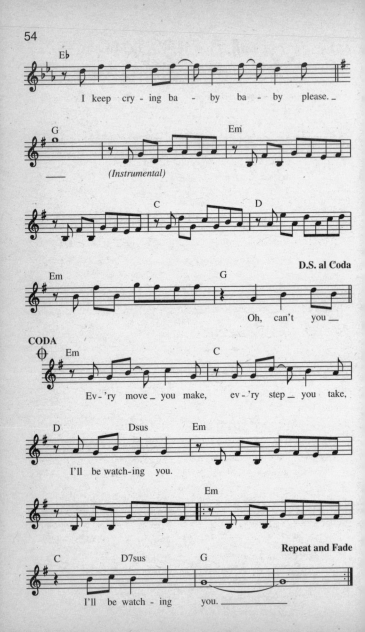

I keep cry - ing ba - by ba - by please.

(Instrumental)

D.S. al Coda

Oh, can't you

CODA

Ev - 'ry move _ you make,   ev - 'ry step _ you take,

I'll be watch-ing you.

Repeat and Fade

I'll be watch - ing   you.

FROM A DISTANCE

Words and Music by
JULIE GOLD

Moderately slow

From a dis-tance the world looks blue and green, and the
dis-tance we all have e - nough, and
dis-tance you look like my friend, e - ven

snow - capped moun - tains white. From a
no one is in need. There are
though we are at war. From a

Play 1st time only

dis-tance the o - cean meets the stream, and the

Play 2nd and 3rd times only

no guns, no bombs, no dis-eas - es, no
dis-tance I can't com - pre-hend what

ea - gle takes to flight. From a
hun - gry mouths to feed. From a
all this war is for. From a

56

From a

CODA

heart _____ of ev - 'ry _____

man. It's the hope of __ hopes, _____ it's the

love of __ loves, _____ it's the song of ev - 'ry

man.

FAITH

Words and Music by
GEORGE MICHAEL

Brightly, with a beat

Well, I guess it would be nice
by,
Instrumental

if I could touch your bod - y.
I know you're ask - ing me to stay.

I know not ev - 'ry - bod - y
Say please, please, please don't go a - way.

has got a bod - y like you. Oh,
You say I'm giv - ing you the blues.

but I got - ta think twice
May - be

be - fore I give my heart a - way.
you mean ev - 'ry word you say.

And   I   know   all   the   games ― you play
Can't   help   but   think   of   yes - ter - day

be - cause   I   play   them   too. ―
        and   an-oth-er   who   tied   me   down to ―

Oh   but   I   need   some ―   time ―
lov - er - boy rules.   } Be - fore   this ―   riv -
Instrumental ends

― off   from   that   e -   mo -
- er   be - comes   an ―   o -

- tion, ―   time   to   pick ― my   heart ―
- cean, ―   be - fore   you   throw ― my   heart ―

― up   off ―   the   floor. ―
― back   on ―   the   floor, ―

Oh,   when   that   love   comes ― down ―
oh,   oh, ba - by,   I'll   re - con - sid -

C   G/B   Am

__ we'll have de - vo -
\- er my fool - ish __ no -

Dm7

\- tion. Well, it takes a strong man, ba -
\- tion. Well, I need some - one __ to hold _

To Coda ⊕ G

\- by, but I'm show - in' you __ the door
__ me but I wait for some - thing more.

N.C.   C

'cause I got - ta have Faith. }
Yes, I got - ta have Faith. }

I got - ta have Faith, __

|1

be - cause I got - ta have Faith,

I got - ta have Faith, Faith, Faith,

ah!   Ba -   Faith,   Faith,   Faith.

D.S. al Coda

I   got - ta have   Faith,   Faith,   Faith.

CODA

G

wait   for some - thing   more...

N.C.   C

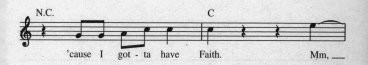

'cause I got - ta have   Faith.   Mm, —

—   I   got - ta   have   Faith, —

be - cause I got - ta have   Faith,   Faith,   Faith.

I   got - ta have Faith,   Faith,   Faith,   ah!

FOOTLOOSE

Theme from the Paramount Motion Picture FOOTLOOSE

Words by DEAN PITCHFORD and KENNY LOGGINS
Music by KENNY LOGGINS

Fast Rock and Roll

1. I been work - in' so hard; I'm punch-in'
2. *(See additional lyrics)*

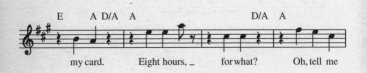

my card. Eight hours, _ for what? Oh, tell me

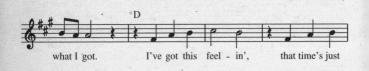

what I got. I've got this feel - in', that time's just

hold - in' me down. _ I'll hit the

ceil - in', or else I'll tear up this town. _

F#m7   Gdim   E/G#

To-night I got-ta cut

Chorus

A   D/A A   D   A

loose,   foot-loose,   kick off your Sun-day shoes.   {Ooh __

D/A   A   D

Please,   Lou - ise,   pull me off __ of my
ee,   Ma - rie,   shake it, shake it for

A   D/A A   D

knees.   Jack,   get back,   come on be-fore we
me.   Whoa,   Mi - lo,   come on, come on let's

A   D/A   A

crack. }   Lose   your   blues,
go. }

1
G   D   A

2
A

ev-'ry-bod-y cut foot - loose.   loose.

Additional Lyrics

2. You're playin' so cool
Obeyin' every rule.
Dig way down in your heart;
You're burnin', yearnin' for some...
Somebody to tell you
That life ain't a-passin' you by.
I'm tryin' to tell you
It will if you don't even try.
You can fly if you'd only cut...
Chorus

FREEZE FRAME

Words and Music by SETH JUSTMAN
and PETER WOLF

66

Stop time heart from then, _____ she's not mine. _____
This freeze frame mo - ment can't be wrong. _____

Solo ends }

(Instrumental)

Freeze, frame, freeze frame. Freeze, frame, freeze frame.

Freeze frame, freeze frame. Freeze frame, and I freeze.

To Coda ⊕

(Instrumental)

GLORIA

Words and Music by
VAN MORRISON

G - L - O - R - I - A___
a)   (Glo   -   ri -

al - right   one   time.___
a)   (Glo   -   ri -

a)   (Glo   -   ri -

a)   *(Instrumental)*

Yeah, she comes a - round___

HOW AM I SUPPOSED TO LIVE WITHOUT YOU

Words and Music by MICHAEL BOLTON
and DOUG JAMES

Slowly

I could hard - ly be - lieve _____ it when I
I'm too proud for cry - ing, did - n't

heard the news _ to - day. _____ I
come here to break down. It's just a

had to come _ and get it straight _ from you. _____
dream of mine _ is com - in' to _____ an end.

They said you are leav - in', some - one's
And how can I blame _____ you when I

swept your heart _ a - way. _____ From the
built my world _ a - round _____ the hope that one

72

look up-on _ your face _ I see it's true. _____ So
_ day we'd be so much more than friends? _

tell me all a-bout it, tell me 'bout the plans you're mak-
I don't want to know the price _ I'm gon-na pay for dream-

- in', _____ oh, ___
- in', _____ oh, ___

tell me one thing more _____ be-fore _ I go. _
e-ven now it's more _____ than I can take. _

_____ } Tell me, how am I __ sup-posed _ to live _ with-out _

_____ you, ___ now that I've been _ lov-in' you _ so

long? _____ How am I __ sup-posed _ to live _____

74

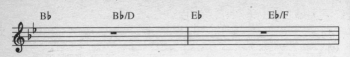

Bb   Bb/D   Eb   Eb/F

Gm7   F/A   B/F#   F#   F#/E

Now

B/D#

I don't wan-na know the price __ I'm gon-na pay for dream-

Emaj7   B/D#

- in', _____ oh, _____

C#m7   G#m7   B/D#

now that your ___ dream has come true. __

C#m7   F#7sus

_____ Tell me,

Emaj7   F#/E

how am I ___ sup-posed ___ to live __ with-out __

GOOD LOVIN'

Words and Music by RUDY CLARK
and ARTHUR RESNICK

_____ yeah yeah. All you
(All you need,)

real-ly need _____ good love." { 'Cause you
Come on,

got-ta have love. Good love, all you need _
give me that love. Good love, all I need _

To Coda ⊕

_____ is love. Good love. } Good, good lov-
_____ is love. Good love. }

- in', ba - by, good love.

1
So come on

2
(scat on "doo's")

Good

love.   Good, good lov - in', ba - by, good

GOOD VIBRATIONS

Words and Music by BRIAN WILSON
and MIKE LOVE

HAPPY TOGETHER

Words and Music by GARY BONNER
and ALAN GORDON

HEY JUDE

Words and Music by JOHN LENNON
and PAUL McCARTNEY

I CAN'T HELP MYSELF
(Sugar Pie, Honey Bunch)

Words and Music by BRIAN HOLLAND,
LAMONT DOZIER and EDWARD HOLLAND

Moderately fast

Sug - ar pie, hon - ey bunch, you know that I
Sug - ar pie, hon - ey bunch, I'm weak - er than a

love you. I can't
man should be. I can't

help my - self, I love you and
help my - self, I'm a fool in

no - bod - y else. Wan - na
love you see.

In and out my life
tell you I don't love you, tell

you come and you go,
you that we're through, and I've tried.

88

(Instrumental)

Can't

help   my - self, __   no ___ I   can't

help   my - self.

D.C. al Coda

CODA

__   I   call   your   name,   girl, __

__   it   starts   the   flame   burn -

- ing   in   my   heart,   tear -

- ing   it   all   a - part.   No   mat -

- ter how I try,   my love ___   I can - not hide.   'Cause

C

Sug - ar   pie,   hon - ey bunch,   you know that I'm
Sug - ar   pie,   hon - ey bunch,   do an - y - thing you

G

weak   for   you. ___   Can't
ask   me   to. ___   Can't

Dm

help   my - self, _____   I   love ___ you and
help   my - self, _____   I   want ___ you and

F   G   **Repeat and Fade**

no - bod - y   else.
no - bod - y   else.

(Everything I Do)
I DO IT FOR YOU

from the Motion Picture ROBIN HOOD: PRINCE OF THIEVES

Words and Music by BRYAN ADAMS, ROBERT JOHN LANGE
and MICHAEL KAMEN

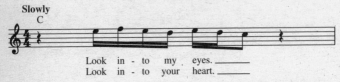

Look in-to my eyes. _____
Look in-to your heart. _____

You will see ____ what you mean to ____
You will find ____ there's noth - in' there to ____

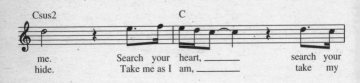

me. Search your heart, _____ search your
hide. Take me as I am, _____ take my

soul, _____ and when you
life. _____ I would

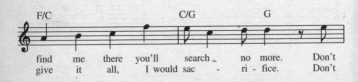

find me there you'll search _ no more. Don't
give it all, I would sac - ri - fice. Don't

92

no - where _____ un - less you're there   all   the

time, _____   all   the

way _   yeah. _____   *(Instrumental)*

1

2

Oh   you can't   tell   me   it's not worth try - in'

for.   I can't   help __ it, there's noth - in' I want

more.   Yeah _ I would fight   for   you. __   I'd

lie ___ for you, ___ walk the wire for you, ___ yeah ___ I'd

die for ___ you. ___ You know it's

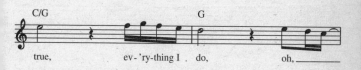

true, ev-'ry-thing I do, oh, ___

___ I do it for ___

you. (Instrumental)

Repeat and Fade
(Vocal ad lib.)

I GOT YOU
(I Feel Good)

Words and Music by
JAMES BROWN

(Instrumental)   Wow!___

___   I feel   nice,___ ___
                                           (Instrumental)

When   I

hold   you   in   my   arms   I

know that I can't do   no   wrong; _____   and

96

I JUST CALLED TO SAY I LOVE YOU

Words and Music by
STEVIE WONDER

1. No New Year's Day to cel - e - brate; no choc - 'late cov - ered can - dy hearts to give a way.
2. rain; no flow - ers bloom; no wed - ding Sat - ur - day with - in the month of June.

No first of spring; no song to sing. In fact here's
But what it is is some - thing true, made up of

3., 4. *(See additional lyrics)*

just an-oth - er or - di - nar - y day.
these three words _ that I _

_ No A - pril

_ must say _ to you. _

I just called _ to say _

_ I love _ you. _

I just called _ to say _

_ how much _ I care. _

I just called ___ to say ___ I love _____ you. ___ And I mean __ it from __ the bot- -tom of ___ my _____ heart. I just called ___ to say __ I love __ you. _ I just called _ to say ___ how much I care. _ I just called _ to say _

Bb7   Cm7

I love _____ you. ___

And I   mean ___   it   from ___   the   bot -

Bb7   Eb   Cb

- tom   of ___   my   heart,   of   my

Db(add2)   Eb

heart,   of   my   heart. _____

(Instrumental)

Additional Lyrics

3. No summer's high; no warm July;
   No harvest moon to light one tender August night.
   No autumn breeze; no falling leaves,
   Not even time for birds to fly to southern skies.

4. No Libra sun; no Halloween;
   No giving thanks to all the Christmas joy you bring.
   But what it is, though old so new
   To fill your heart like no three words could ever do.
   (To Chorus:)

I WRITE THE SONGS

Words and Music by
BRUCE JOHNSTON

Slowly

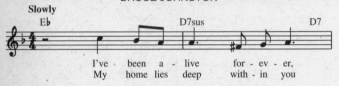

I've been a-live for-ev-er,
My home lies deep with-in you

and I wrote the ver-y first song. ___
and I've got my own place in your soul.

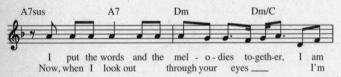

I put the words and the mel-o-dies to-geth-er, I am
Now, when I look out through your eyes ___ I'm

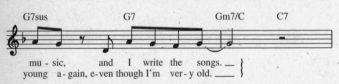

mu-sic, and I write the songs. ___ }
young a-gain, e-ven though I'm ver-y old. ___ }

I write the songs ___ that make the whole world sing;

I write the songs ___ of love and spe-cial things. ___

IMAGINE

Words and Music by
JOHN LENNON

G7

Ah.

C   Cmaj7   F

I-mag-ine there's   no coun - tries.
                              sions.

C   Cmaj7

It is - n't hard _____ to   do. _____
      I won - der if you _____ can. _____

F   C   Cmaj7

_____   Noth-ing to kill __ or die __
_____   No need for greed _ or hun -

F   C   3   Cmaj7

_____ for   and no re - li - gion, _ too. _
- ger,   a broth-er - hood _____ of man. _

F   Am/E

_____   I - mag - ine all   the peo -
_____   I - mag - ine all   the peo -

Dm7   F/C   G   C/G

ple _____   liv - ing   life   in peace. _
ple _____   shar - ing   all   the world. _

107

IF YOU LEAVE ME NOW

Words and Music by
PETER CETERA

Lyrics (beneath staves):

A love ___ like ours ___ is love ___
We've come ___ too far ___ to leave ___

___ that's hard ___ to find. _____
___ it all ___ be - hind. _____

How could we let ___ it ___ slip ___ a - way? ___
How could we end ___ it ___ all ___ this way? ___

_____

_____ When to - mor - row comes, then we'll both ___

___ re - gret ___ the things we said ___ to - day. ___

_____ *(Instrumental)*

Chord symbols:
F9sus · Bbm/F · F · Am7 · F · G · 1,3 C · Am7 · E7 · 2,4 C · Em7 · Am7 · Dm · Em · Fm · To Coda ⊕

110

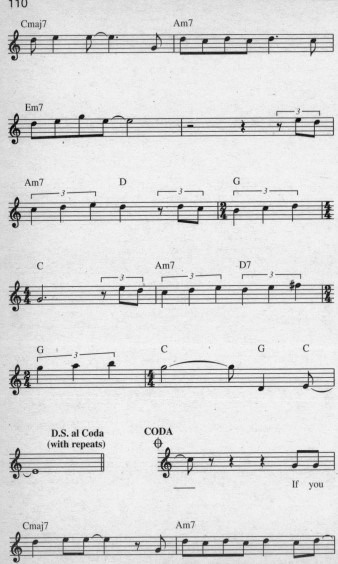

D.S. al Coda
(with repeats)

CODA

If you

leave me now, ___ you'll take a - way the big - gest part ___

ISLAND GIRL

Words and Music by ELTON JOHN
and BERNIE TAUPIN

114

like a well worn tire. _____

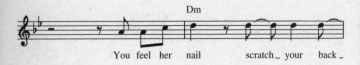

You feel her nail scratch __ your back __

__ just like __ a rake, _____.

oh, _____ he one more gone, __ he one __

__ more john __ who make __ de mis - take. __

D.S. al Coda **CODA**

Is - land   white man's. __

Repeat and Fade

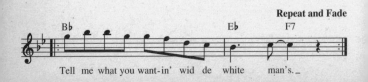

Tell me what you want-in' wid de white man's. __

JACK AND DIANE

Words and Music by
JOHN MELLENCAMP

Moderate 2

A little dit-ty a-bout

Jack and Di - ane, _____

two A-mer-i-can kids grow-in' up

in the heart - land.

Jack, he's gon-na be _____ a

foot - ball star; _____

116

Di - ane deb - u - tante, back seat

of Jack - y's car. *(Instrumental)*

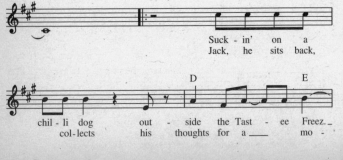

chil - li dog out - side the Tast - ee Freez.
col - lects his thoughts for a ____ mo -

Suck - in' on a
Jack, he sits back,

117

life goes __ on, _____

long af - ter the thrill of

liv - ing is __ gone. __ Say - in',

oh yeah, __ life goes __ on, __

_____ long af - ter the

To Coda ⊕

thrill of liv - ing is __ gone. __

1

__ Now, walk on. *(Instrumental)*

119

Oh, let it rock,

let   it   roll. _____

Let the Bi - ble belt   come and

save   my   soul. _____

Hold - in' on   to   six - teen   as

long   as   you   can. _____

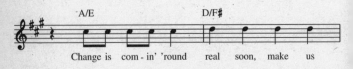

Change is com - in' 'round   real soon, make us

wom - en and men.

A lit - tle dit - ty a - bout

Jack and Di - ane, _____

two A - mer - i - can kids do - in' the

best that they __ can.

(Instrumental)

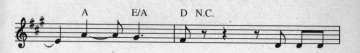

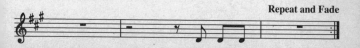

Repeat and Fade

JOY TO THE WORLD

Words and Music by
HOYT AXTON

Moderate Gospel Rock

Jer - e - mi - ah was a bull - frog,
If I were the king of the world,
know I love the la - dies,

was a good friend of mine.
tell you what I'd do.
love to have my fun. I'm a

Nev - er un - der-stood a sin - gle word he said, _ but I
Throw a - way the cars and the bars and the wars, and
high night fly - er and a rain-bow rid - er, a

helped him a - drink - in' his wine. ___ Yes he
make sweet love to you. ___ Yes I'd
straight shoot - in' son - of - a - gun. ___ Yes a

al - ways had some might - y fine wine.
make sweet love to you. ___
straight shoot - in' son - of - a - gun. ___ Sing - ing

joy to the world, all _____ the boys and

123

girls _ now.   Joy   to   the fish - es in the

To Coda ⊕

deep blue sea. _   Joy   to _   you and   me. _

(Instrumental)

D.C. al Coda   CODA

You _   Joy _ to _

124

the world, all the

boys and girls. Joy to

the world, joy to

you and me. Joy to the

world, all the boys and girls.

Joy to the fish - es in the deep blue sea.

Repeat and Fade

Joy to you and me.

LADY IN RED

Words and Music by
CHRIS DeBURGH

Moderately slow

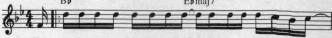

I've nev-er seen you look-ing so love-ly as you did _ to-night;_
nev-er seen you look-ing so gor-geous as you did _ to-night;_

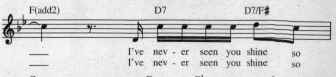

_
_
I've nev-er seen you shine so
I've nev-er seen you shine so

bright. Mm mm mm. _ I've
bright. You were a-maz-ing. I've

nev-er seen so man-y men ask _ you if you want-ed to dance._
nev-er seen so man-y want to be _ there _ by _ your side, _

_ They're look-ing for a lit-tle ro-mance, giv-en half _ a
_ and when you turn to me and smiled, it took my breath _ a-

chance. I have nev-er seen that dress you're wear-ing, or the
way. I have nev-er had _ such a feel-ing, such a

high-lights in _ your hair _ that catch _ your eyes. _ I have _ been blind. _
feel-ing of _ com-plete _ and ut - ter love. _ As I do to-night. _

JUST THE WAY YOU ARE

Words and Music by
BILLY JOEL

Moderately

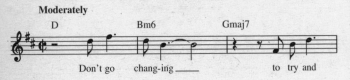

Don't go chang-ing _____ to try and

please me _____ you nev-er

let me down _____ be-fore _____

mm _____ mm. Don't i-mag-

-ine you're too fa-mil-

-iar _____ and I don't see

129

130

_ times _   I'll take you   Just _

_ The Way _   You Are. _   Don't go

try - ing _   some _ new fash -

- ion _   don't change the col -

- or   of   your   hair _

mm _____ mm. _____ You al - ways

have   my   un - spok - en pas - sion _

131

132

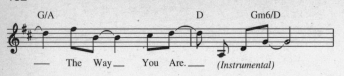

The Way You Are. *(Instrumental)*

I need to know

that you will al - ways be

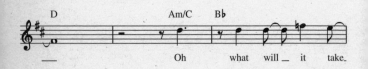

the same old some - one that I knew.

Oh what will it take

till you be - lieve in me

134

bet - ter ___ I love you Just ___

___ The Way ___ You Are. ___ *(Instrumental)*

D.S. al Coda **CODA**

I don't ___ want

clev - er _____ con - ver - sa-

- tion I nev - er

LA BAMBA

By RITCHIE VALENS

Yo no soy mar - i - ne - ro.

Yo no soy mar - i - ne - ro, soy cap - i - tan;

yo no soy mar - i - ne - ro, soy cap - i - tan.

To Coda ⊕

Bam - ba bam - ba,

bam - ba bam - ba,

bam - ba, bam - ba,

D.S. al Coda

bam - ba bam... Pa - ra bai - lar la bam -

CODA
⊕

Repeat and Fade

Bam - ba, bam - ba!

LIKE A VIRGIN

Words and Music by BILLY STEINBERG
and TOM KELLY

Oooh, _____

oooh, _____ oooh. _____

D.S. al Coda

You're so fine. __

CODA

next to __ mine. __ Like a vir - gin. Ooh, __ ooh, __ like a

vir - gin. Feels so good __ in - side __

_____ when you hold me and your

Repeat and Fade

heart beats and you love me.

LOUIE, LOUIE

Words and Music by
RICHARD BERRY

LIMBO ROCK

Words and Music by BILLY STRANGE and JON SHELDON

Bright Latin Rock

Ev - 'ry lim - bo boy __ and girl
spread your lim - bo feet,
self a lim - bo girl,

all a - round the lim - bo world,
then you move to lim - bo beat.
give that chick a lim - bo whirl.

gon - na do the Lim - bo Rock
Lim - bo an - kle, lim - bo knee;
There's a lim - bo moon, __ a - bove,

all a - round the lim - bo clock. }
bend back, like the lim - bo tree. }
you will fall in lim - bo love. }

Jack be lim - bo, Jack __ be quick,

Jack go un - der lim - bo stick.

All a - round the lim - bo clock,

hey, let's do the Lim - bo Rock.

1, 2
G6

Spoken: "Limbo lower now, limbo lower now.

How low can you go?"

{ First you
{ Get your -

3
G6

Spoken: "Don't move that limbo bar. You'll be a limbo star.

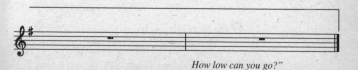

How low can you go?"

LIVIN' ON A PRAYER

Words and Music by DESMOND CHILD,
JON BON JOVI and RICHIE SAMBORA

half - way there. ___ Whoa, ___ liv -

- in' on a prayer. ___ Take my ___ hand, ___ we'll

make it, I swear. ___ Whoa, ___ liv -

- in' on a prayer. ___

Liv - in' on ___ a prayer. _

(Instrumental)

MAGGIE MAY

**Words and Music by ROD STEWART
and MARTIN QUITTENTON**

Medium Rock beat

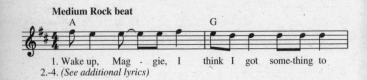

1. Wake up, Mag - gie, I   think I   got   some-thing to
2.-4. *(See additional lyrics)*

say to you. ___   It's

late Sep - tem-ber and I   real - ly should _ be   back _

___ at ___ school. ___   I

know I   keep you a - mused, _   but I

149

feel I'm being used. ___ Oh,

Mag-gie, I could-n't have tried ___ an-y

more. _____ You

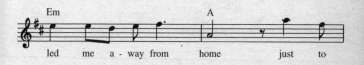
led me a-way from home just to

save you from being a - lone. You

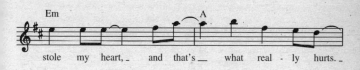
stole my heart, __ and that's __ what real-ly hurts. __

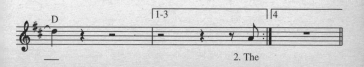
___   2. The

(Instrumental)

Repeat and Fade

Additional Lyrics

2. The morning sun, when it's in your face,
   Really shows your age.
   But that don't worry me none.
   In my eyes, you're everything.
   I laughed at all of your jokes.
   My love you didn't need to coax.
   Oh, Maggie, I couldn't have tried any more.
   You led me away from home
   Just to save you from being alone.
   You stole my soul, and that's a pain I can do without.

3. All I needed was a friend
   To lend a guiding hand.
   But you turned into a lover, and, mother, what a lover!
   You wore me out.
   All you did was wreck my bed,
   And, in the morning, kick me in the head.
   Oh, Maggie, I couldn't have tried any more.
   You led me away from home
   'Cause you didn't want to be alone.
   You stole my heart. I couldn't leave you if I tried.

4. I suppose I could collect my books
   And get on back to school.
   Or steal my daddy's cue
   And make a living out of playing pool.
   Or find myself a rock 'n' roll band
   That needs a helping hand.
   Oh, Maggie, I wish I'd never seen your face.
   You made a first-class fool out of me.
   But I'm as blind as a fool can be.
   You stole my heart, but I love you anyway.

SHOUT

**Words and Music by O'KELLY ISLEY,
RONALD ISLEY and RUDOLPH ISLEY**

Bm   D   Bm

will.)   Say that you, __ (Say you will.)

D   Bm

(Say!) say that you love me. (Say!) Say that you need me.

D   Bm   N.C.

Say __ that you want me. Say you wan-na please me.

Eb   Cm

(Say!) Come on __ now. __ (Say!) Come on __ now. __

Eb   Cm - N.C.

(Say!) Come on __ now. __ (Say!) I still re -

Eb

mem-ber when I used to be __ nine years old, __

Cm

__ hey __ yeah. __ And I was a fool __

Eb

__ for you from the bot-tom of my

soul, ___ yeah ___ yeah. ___ Now that I found ___

___ you, I will nev - er let you

go, ___ no ___ no. ___ And if you ev - er

leave me, you know it's gon - na hurt me

Moderate Shuffle (♩ = ♩ ♪)

so. I want you to

know, I said, I want you to know ___

___ right now. You been good ___ to me

sis - ters, much bet - ter than I been to my - self,

so good,___ so good.___ And if ___ you ev - er leave___

___ me, ___ I don't want no - bod - y else,___

Eb

___ hey, hey. I said, I want you to know,___

___ yeah, I said, I want you to know___

Lively Rock (Tempo I)

N.C.

___ right now. ___ You know you make me wan-na

E   **C#m**

(Shout!) pick my heels _ up and (Shout!) throw my hands _ up and

E   **C#m**

(Shout!) throw my head _ back and (Shout!) come on ___ now.

E   **C#m**

(Shout!) Come on ___ now. (Shout!) Play it, Sis-ter Al-len, ___ hey.

155

156

(Shout!) (Spoken:) *All right now, come on, basses.* Bum, bum, bum, bum,

bum, bum, bum, bum, bum, bum, bum, bum, bum,

bum, bum, bum, bum, bum, bum. Come on __ now. _

Come on __ now. _____

Shoo-be - do-wop do wop, wop, wop, wop.

Shoo-be-do-be do-wop do wop, do wop, wop, wop.

Shout, shout, shout, woh. _

Shout, shout, shout, whoa. _ Hey, _____

(Hey,) _____ hey. _____

_____ (You know you make me wan-na shout!)

Kick my heels_ up and

(Shout!) throw my hands_ up and (Shout!) throw my head_ back and

(Shout!) come on __ now. ___ Don't for-get to say you will._

_____ Don't for-get to say yeah, yeah,_ yeah, yeah,_ yeah.

Say you will

Say you

will.

will. *(Spoken:) Now wait a minute.*

All right, who was that? You know you make me wan-na shout.

MONY, MONY

Words and Music by BOBBY BLOOM, TOMMY JAMES,
RITCHIE CORDELL and BO GENTRY

MORE THAN WORDS

Words and Music by NUNO BETTENCOURT
and GARY CHERONE

Moderate Rock

Say - in', "I ____ love ____ you" is
Now that I've ____ tried ____ to

not the words ____ I want ____ to ____ hear ____ from you. ____
talk to you ____ and make ____ you ____ un - der - stand. ____

____ It's not that I ____ want ____ you
____ All ____ you ____ have to do is

not to say. ____ But if ____ you on - ly ____ knew ____
close your eyes ____ and just ____ reach out ____ your ____ hands. ____

____ how eas - y ____
____ and touch me, ____

it would be ____ to show ____ me how ____ you feel, ____
hold me close, ____ don't ev - er let ____ me go. ____

CODA

- in', "I ___ love ___ you."___

La di da ___ da di da ___ di dai dai ___ da. ___

More ___ than ___ words. ___ More ___ than ___

words. ___ Ooh, ___

Ooh. ___

___ More than ___ words. ___

MY GIRL

Words and Music by WILLIAM "SMOKEY" ROBINSON
and RONALD WHITE

I've got sun-shine ___ on a cloud - y

day; When it's cold out-side,

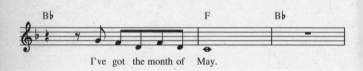

I've got the month of May.

I guess you say, what can make me

feel this way? My girl, _____ talk-ing 'bout

my ___ girl. _____ I've got

so much hon-ey, the bees en-vy me;

I've got a sweet-er song _____

than the birds in the tree. Well,

I guess you say, what can make me

feel this way? My girl, _____ talk-ing 'bout

my___ girl._____ I don't

need no mon-ey, for-tune or fame.

I've got all the rich-es, ba - by,

one man can claim. Well,

I guess you say, what can make me

feel this way? My girl,_____ talk-ing 'bout

my __ girl. _____   I've got sun-shine on a

cloud - y day __ with my girl; _____   I've

e - ven got the month of May with my girl. _____

Talk-ing 'bout, _ talk-ing 'bout, _ talk-ing 'bout _

my girl. _____   Woo! ____   My girl. __

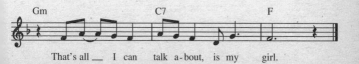

That's all __ I can talk a-bout, is my girl.

MY HEART WILL GO ON

(Love Theme from 'Titanic')
from the Paramount and Twentieth Century Fox
Motion Picture TITANIC

Music by JAMES HORNER
Lyric by WILL JENNINGS

169

170

171

NO WOMAN NO CRY

Words and Music by
VINCENT FORD

Moderately slow

No wom-an, no cry.

No wom-an, no cry.

{ No wom-an, no cry. }
{ Here __ lit-tle dar-lin', don't shed no tears. }

No wom-an, no cry. Said, said,

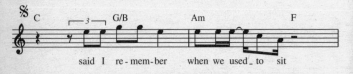

said I re-mem-ber when we used to sit

in the gov-ern-ment yard in Trench-town.

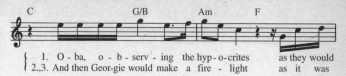

C   G/B   Am   F

1. O - ba,   o - b - serv - ing the hyp - o - crites   as they would
2.,3. And then Geor - gie would make a fire - light   as it was

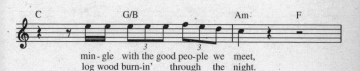

C   G/B   Am   F

min - gle with the good peo - ple we   meet,
log wood burn - in'   through   the   night.

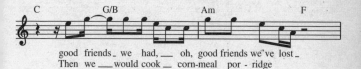

C   G/B   Am   F

good friends _ we had, __ oh, good friends we've lost _
Then we __ would cook __ corn-meal por - ridge

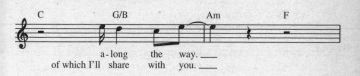

C   G/B   Am   F

a - long   the   way. __
of which I'll share   with   you. __

C   G/B

In __ this bright _ fu - ture   you _
My   feet __ is   my

Am   F

__ can't   for - get   your _ past
on - ly __ car - riage, _

so, dry your tears _ I ____ say.   And
so, I've got to push on ____ through, but while I'm gone I mean...

Ev-'ry-thing's gon-na be al-right.   Ev-'ry-thing's gon-na be al-right.

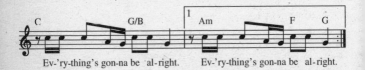

Ev-'ry-thing's gon-na be al-right.   Ev-'ry-thing's gon-na be al-right.

Ev - 'ry-thing's gon - na be al - right   so,

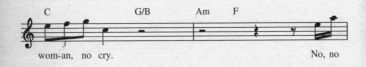

wom-an, no cry.   No, no

wom - an, no   wom - an, no cry.

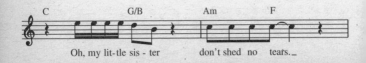

Oh, my lit-tle sis - ter   don't shed no tears. _

D.S. al Coda

No wom-an, no cry.

CODA

No wom-an, no cry.

No wom-an, no cry.

Oh, my lit-tle dar-lin', I say don't shed no tears.

No wom-an, no cry. Yeah.

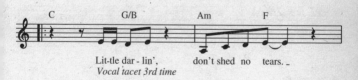

Lit-tle dar-lin', don't shed no tears.
Vocal tacet 3rd time

Repeat and Fade

No wom-an, no cry.

PHILADELPHIA FREEDOM

Words and Music by ELTON JOHN
and BERNIE TAUPIN

Moderately

1. I used to be a roll - ing stone, you know
2. *(See additional lyrics)*

if the cause was right I'd leave

to find the an - swer on the road.

I used to be a heart beat-ing

for some - one. But the times have changed

the less I say the more

my work gets done.

Chorus

'Cause I live and breathe this Phil - a - del - phi - a Free - dom

From the day that I was born I waved the flag.

Phil - a - del - phia Free - dom took me knee - high to a man.

Yeah! Gave me peace of mind my dad - dy nev - er had.

Oh, Phil - a - del - phi - a Free -

D.S. al Coda

Oh

CODA

Gm7   Bb Am7 Gm7

Don't you know I love - ove - ove___ you.

Bb   Am7   Gm7

Don't you know I   love - ove - ove ___

___ you   yes I   do. ___

F

(Phil - a - del - phi - a   Free - dom)   I

Bb   Am7   Gm7

love - ove - ove ___ you, yes I do. ___

F   **Repeat and Fade**

___ (Phil - a - del - phi - a   Free - dom) Don't you know that I

Additional Lyrics

2. If you choose to, you can live your life alone
   Some people choose the city,
   Some others choose the good old family home
   I like living easy without family ties
   'Til the whippoorwill of freedom zapped me
   Right between the eyes.
   Chorus

RESPECT

Words and Music by
OTIS REDDING

Moderate Rock

What you want ba-by I got.
I ain't gon-na do you wrong while you gone.

What you need you know I got it.
I ain't gon-na do you wrong 'cause I don't wan-na.

All I'm ask-in' is for a lit-tle re-

spect, when you come home. Ba-

-by, when you come home, __ re-

spect. I'm out __ to give you
Ooh, __ your kiss-es,

all my mon-ey. But all I'm ask-in'
sweet-er than hon-ey. But guess what,

F   G

in re - turn, hon - ey,   is to give me
so here's my mon - ey.   All I want you to do for me

F

my   pro - per re - spect }
is   give me some here } when you get

C   F

home.   Yeah, ba - by,   when you get

C7

home.   (Just a lit - tle bit.

F   C7

Just a lit - tle bit.)   R - E - S - P - E - C - T,

F

find out what it means to me,

C7   F

R - E - S - P - E - C - T,   take out T - C - P.

Repeat and Fade

C7   F

A lit - tle re - spect.

SHOW ME THE WAY

Words and Music by
PETER FRAMPTON

Bm

There has to be ___ a force.
There has to be ___ a fool ___
I can't be - lieve ___ this is

Bb

Who do ___ I phone? ___
to play ___ my part. ___
hap - pen - ing ___ to me. ___

A7sus

The stars are out ___ and shin -
Some - one thought ___ of heal -
I watch you when ___ you're sleep -

G7

- ing, but all I real - ly want ___ to know, ___
- ing, but all I real - ly want ___ to know, ___
- ing, and then I want to take ___ your love, ___

To Coda ⊕

Bm

oh, won't ___ you ___

G

___ show me the way?

Bm

I want ___ you; ___

SMELLS LIKE TEEN SPIRIT

Words and Music by KURT COBAIN,
CHRIS NOVOSELIC and DAVID GROHL

(Sittin' On)
THE DOCK OF THE BAY

Words and Music by STEVE CROPPER
and OTIS REDDING

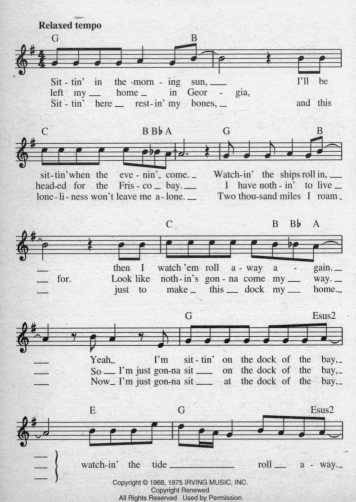

SMOOTH

Words by ROB THOMAS
Music by ROB THOMAS and ITAAL SHUR

Medium Latin Rock

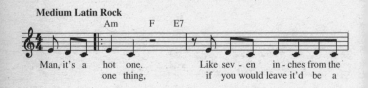

Man, it's a hot one. Like sev - en in - ches from the
one thing, if you would leave it'd be a

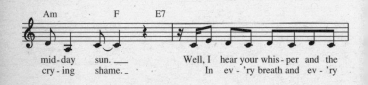

mid - day sun. ___ Well, I hear your whis - per and the
cry - ing shame. ___ In ev - 'ry breath and ev - 'ry

words melt ev - 'ry - one. But you stay so ___
word I hear ___ your ___ name call - ing me

___ cool. ___ My Mu - ñe -
___ out. ___ Out from the

qui - ta, my Span - ish Har - lem Mo - na
bar - ri - o, you hear my rhy - thm on your

Li - sa.   Well, you're my rea - son _ for _
ra - di - o.   You feel the turn - ing of the

_ rea - son, _   the _ step in
world so soft and slow;   turn - ing me

my   groove. _ }
round and round. _ }   And if you said _

_ this life ain't good e - nough, I would give

my   world   to lift you up. I could change

my   life   to bet - ter suit _ your _ mood. _

_   'cause you're so _

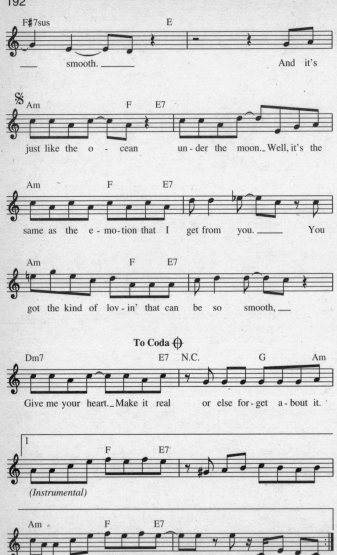

F#7sus   E

_ smooth. _____   And it's

% Am   F   E7

just like the o - cean   un - der the moon.. Well, it's the

Am   F   E7

same as the e - mo - tion that I   get from you. ____   You

Am   F   E7

got the kind of lov - in' that can   be   so   smooth, _

To Coda ⊕

Dm7   E7 N.C.   G   Am

Give me your heart._ Make it real   or else for - get a - bout it.

[1]

F   E7

(Instrumental)

Am .   F   E7

                              Well, I'll tell you

SOMEBODY TO LOVE

Words and Music by
DARBY SLICK

196

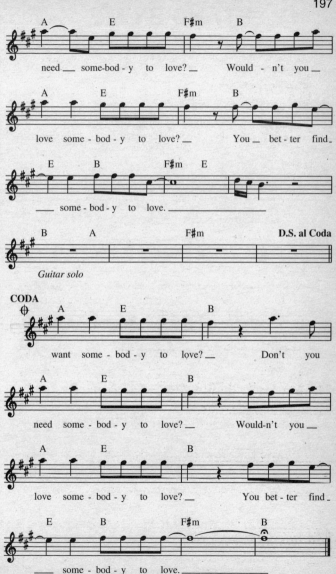

STAND BY ME

Words and Music by BEN E. KING,
JERRY LEIBER and MIKE STOLLER

Moderately, with a beat

STAYIN' ALIVE

from the Motion Picture SATURDAY NIGHT FEVER

Words and Music by BARRY GIBB,
MAURICE GIBB and ROBIN GIBB

Medium Rock beat

We can try __ to un-der-stand __ the

New York Times' __ ef - fect __ on man. __

Fm7

Wheth-er you're a broth-er or wheth - er you're a moth-er, you're Stay-

- in' A - live, __ Stay-in' A - live. __

Feel the cit - y break-in' and ev - 'ry-bod-y shak-in' and we're

Stay-in' A-live, __ Stay-in' A-live. __ Ah, ha, ha, ha,

Stay-in' A-live, __ Stay-in' A-live. __ Ah, ha, ha, ha,

202

Stay-in' A - live. _____

Well now, I __

Life go - in' no - where. __

Some-bod-y help me.___ Some-bod-y help __ me, yeah.

Life go-in' no - where. __

Some-bod-y help __ me, yeah. _ Stay-in' A-live._

D.S. and Fade

_____ Well, you can tell _

TEARS IN HEAVEN

**Words and Music by ERIC CLAPTON
and WILL JENNINGS**

204

SUMMER OF '69

Words and Music by BRYAN ADAMS
and JIM VALLANCE

I got my first real six - string;

bought __ it at the five and dime;

played __ it 'til my fin - gers __ bled;

was the sum - mer of six - ty - nine.

Me __ and some guys from school
Ain't __ no use in com - plain - in'
And __ now the times are chang - in';

had a band and we tried real hard.
when you got a ____ job to do.
look at ev - 'ry - thing that's come and gone.

Bm   A

Those _ were the best days of my ___

D

life. *(Instrumental)*

To Coda ⊕ | 1

A

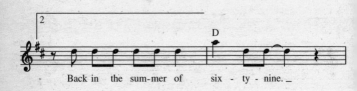

| 2

Back in the sum-mer of six - ty - nine. _

A

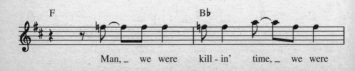

F   Bb

Man, _ we were kill - in' time, _ we were

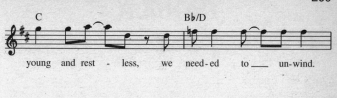

young and rest - less, we need-ed to ___ un-wind.

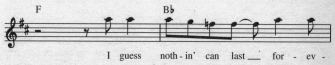

I guess noth-in' can last ___ for - ev -

- er, for - ev - er, _____ no!

(Instrumental)

D.S. al Coda

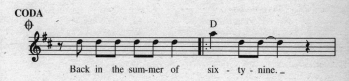

CODA

Back in the sum-mer of six - ty - nine. _

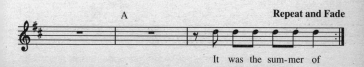

Repeat and Fade

It was the sum-mer of

TEQUILA
By CHUCK RIO

212

(Spoken:) Tequila!

Play 3 times

(Spoken:) Tequila!

TIME IN A BOTTLE

Words and Music by
JIM CROCE

214

215

THREE TIMES A LADY

Words and Music by
LIONEL RICHIE

Slowly

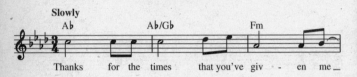

Thanks for the times that you've giv-en me

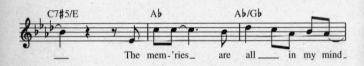

The mem-'ries are all in my mind

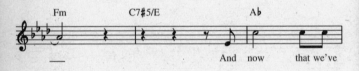

And now that we've

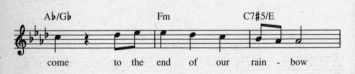

come to the end of our rain-bow

there's some-thing I must say out loud:

You're once,

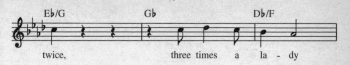

twice, three times a la - dy

and I love____ you.____

__ Yes you're once,__ twice,__

three times a la - dy and I love_

_ you, ____ I love_

____ you. ____

When we are to - geth - er the

mo - ments I cher - ish ___ with ev - 'ry beat ___

___ of my ___ heart, ___ To

touch you, to hold you, to feel you, to

need you, ___ there's noth - ing to keep us a -

part. ___

(Instrumental)

Ooo ___

Eb/Ab   Db/Ab

___ ooo ___   ooo ___   ooo ___

Ab   Eb/Ab   Db/Ab

___ ooo ___   ooo ___

Ab

___   You're once,

Eb/G   Gb   Db/F

twice,   three times ___ a la - dy ___

Bbm7   Ab   Eb

and   I   love ___   you, ___

Eb/Db   Eb/C   Eb/Bb

___   I   love ___

Ab   *8va*

you.   *(Instrumental)*

THRILLER

Words and Music by
ROD TEMPERTON

It's close to mid - night, __ and
You hear the door __ slam __ and
They're out to get __ you. __ There's

some-thin' e - vil's lurk - in' in the dark. __
re - al - ize there's no-where left to run. __
de - mons clos - in' in on ev - 'ry side. __

Un - der the moon - light __ you
You feel the cold __ hand, __ and
They will pos - sess __ you __ un -

see a sight that al - most stops your heart. __
won - der if you'll ev - er see the sun. __
less you change that num - ber on your dial. __

You try to scream, __ but
You close your eyes, __ and
Now is the time __ for

ter - ror takes __ the sound __ be - fore __ you make.
hope that this __ is just __ i - mag - i - na -
you and I __ to cud - dle close __ to - geth -

_ it. _ / You start to freeze_
- tion. _ / But all the while,_
- er. _ / All through the night _

_____ / as hor-ror looks_ you right_be-tween_the eyes. _
_____ / you hear the crea - ture creep-in' up _ be-hind. _
_____ / I'll save you from_the ter - ror on _ the screen._

_ / You're par - a - lyzed. _ / 'Cause this is
_ / You're out of time. _ / 'Cause this is
_ / I'll make you see _ / that this is

thrill - er, _ / thrill - er night, and
thrill - er, _ / thrill - er night. There
thrill - er, _ / thrill - er night, 'cause

no one's gon - na save _ you from the beast_
ain't no sec - ond chance_ a - gainst the thing_
I could thrill you more _ than an - y ghost_

_ a - bout to strike._ You know, it's
_ with for - ty eyes._ You know, it's
_ would dare to try._ Girl, this is

thrill - er, _ / thrill - er night. You're
thrill - er, _ / thrill - er night. You're
thrill - er, _ / thrill - er night, so

To Coda ⊕ | **1**

F#7 · · · A7 · F#7 · A/B

fight-ing for your life __ in - side a kill - er thrill - er to -
fight-ing for your life __ in - side a
let me hold you tight __ and share a

C#m7

night. _____

2

A7 · F#7 · A/B

kill - er thrill - er to -

C#m7 · E · F#7

night. Night crea - tures call and __ the

Amaj9 · B · C#m7

dead start __ to walk in __ their mas - quer-ade. There's __

E/B

__ no __ es-cap - in' the jaws of __ the a - lien __ this

A#m7b5 · Amaj7

time _____ This is __ the end of your
(They're o - pen wide.)

life. _____

CODA

kill - er   thrill - er.

Repeat ad lib.

(See additional lyrics)

Additional Lyrics

Darkness falls across the land.
The midnight hour is close at hand.
Creatures crawl in search of blood
To terrorize y'awl's neighborhood.
And whosoever shall be found
Without the soul for getting down
Must stand and face the hounds of hell
And rot inside a corpse's shell.

The foulest stench is in the air,
The funk of forty thousand years,
And grizzly ghouls from every tomb
Are closing in to seal your doom.
And though you fight to stay alive,
Your body starts to shiver,
For no mere mortal can resist
The evil of a thriller.

THE TWIST

Words and Music by
HANK BALLARD

Rock and Roll shuffle

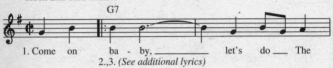

1. Come on ba - by, _____ let's do _ The
2.,3. *(See additional lyrics)*

Twist. Come on ba - by, _____

_ let's do The Twist. Take me by my lit - tle

hand _____ and go _ like this.

Chorus

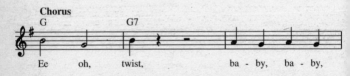

Ee oh, twist, ba - by, ba - by,

twist. ('round and a - round and a - round and a-)

Just, _____ just like

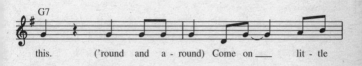

this. ('round and a - round) Come on ___ lit - tle

miss, and do ___ The

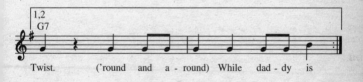

Twist. ('round and a - round) While dad - dy is

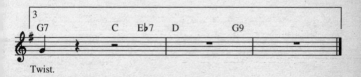

Twist.

Additional Lyrics

2. While daddy is sleeping and mama ain't around.
   While daddy is sleeping and mama ain't around.
   We're gonna twisty, twisty, twisty until we tear the house down.
   Chorus

3. You should see my little sis.
   You should see my little sis.
   She knows how to rock and she knows how to twist.
   Chorus

TWIST AND SHOUT

Words and Music by BERT RUSSELL
and PHIL MEDLEY

Moderately, with a beat

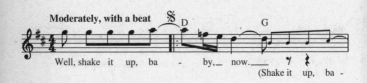

Well, shake it up, ba - by,_ now._
(Shake it up, ba -

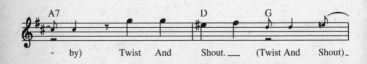

- by) Twist And Shout._ (Twist And Shout)

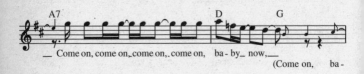

_ Come on, come on, come on, come on, ba - by_ now,_
(Come on, ba -

Come on and work it on out._
- by) (Work it on out)_

1. Well, work it on out, _____ (Work it on out)_
2.,3. You know you twist, lit - tle girl, _____ (Twist lit - tle girl)_

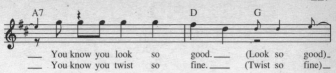

You know you look so good.___ (Look so good)_
You know you twist so fine.___ (Twist so fine)_

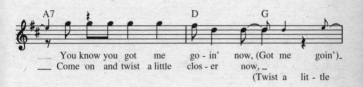

You know you got me go - in' now, (Got me goin')_
Come on and twist a little clos - er now, _
(Twist a lit - tle

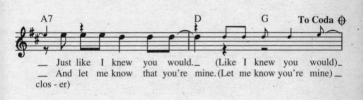

To Coda

Just like I knew you would._ (Like I knew you would)_
And let me know that you're mine. (Let me know you're mine) _
clos - er)

1. A7   2. A7

___ Well, shake it up, ba - _

D   G   A   G   A

(Instrumental)

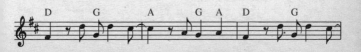

D   G   A   G   A   D   G

228

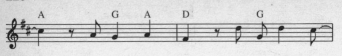

Ah Ah

D.S. al Coda

Ah Ah Ah _____ Shake it up, ba-

CODA

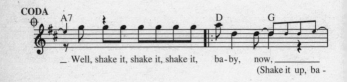

_ Well, shake it, shake it, shake it, ba-by, now, _____

(Shake it up, ba-

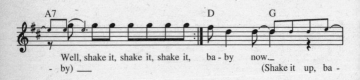

Well, shake it, shake it, shake it, ba-by now._

- by) __

(Shake it up, ba-

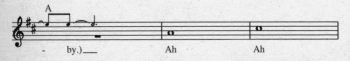

- by.) __ Ah Ah

Ah Ah

(Instrumental)

WAKE UP LITTLE SUSIE

Words and Music by BOUDLEAUX BRYANT
and FELICE BRYANT

we're   in   trou - ble   deep.⎫
rep - u - ta - tion   is   shot.⎭ Wake up __ lit - tle

Su - sie, __   Wake up __ lit - tle

Su - sie. __   Well,

what are we gon - na   tell   your ma - ma? __

What are we gon - na   tell   your pa? __

What are we gon - na   tell   our friends __ when   they   say,

"Ooh   la - la."   Wake up __ lit - tle

Su - sie, __   Wake up __ lit - tle

UNDER THE BOARDWALK

**Words and Music by ARTIE RESNICK
and KENNY YOUNG**

Moderately, with a beat

Oh, when the sun beats down __ and burns the
park you hear __ the hap - py
Instrumental

tar up - on the roof, _____ and your
sound of a car - ou - sel, _____ you can

shoes get so hot you wish your tired feet __ were fire -
al - most taste the hot - dogs and french __ fries

- proof.
they sell.
End instrumental

Un - der the board -

- walk, _ down by the sea,

_____ yeah, on a

blan - ket with my ba - by's _____ where I'll _____

_____ be. (Un - der the board - walk) Out

of the sun _____ we'll be
(Un - der the board - walk)

hav - in' some fun _____ peo - ple
(Un - der the board - walk)

walk - in' a - bove _____ we'll be
(Un - der the board - walk)

fall - in' in love _ un - der the board - walk, board -
(Un - der the board - walk, board -

1,2 | **3**

walk. From the walk.
walk.) *Instrumental* walk.)

WE'VE ONLY JUST BEGUN

Words and Music by ROGER NICHOLS
and PAUL WILLIAMS

235

WHAT'S GOING ON

Words and Music by MARVIN GAYE,
AL CLEVELAND and RENALDO BENSON

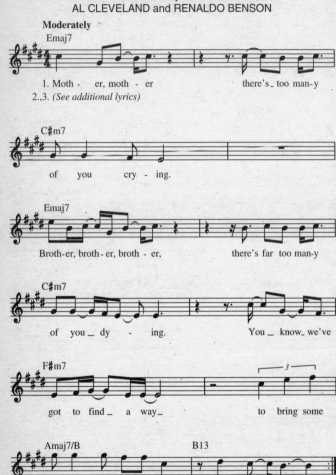

Additional Lyrics

2. Father, father we don't need to escalate
   You see, war is not the answer for only love can conquer hate
   You know we've got to find a way to bring some lovin' here today.
   Chorus

3. Father, father everybody thinks we're wrong
   Oh but, who are they to judge us simply because our hair is long?
   Oh you know we've got to find a way to bring some understanding here today.
   Chorus

YOU'VE GOT A FRIEND

Words and Music by
CAROLE KING

When you're down _____ and trou -
a - bove _____

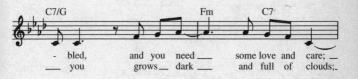

- bled, and you need _____ some love and care;
_____ you grows _____ dark _____ and full of clouds;

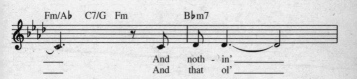

And noth - in' _____
And that ol' _____

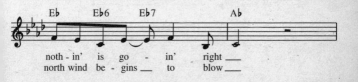

noth - in' is go - in' right _____
north wind be - gins _____ to blow _____

close your eyes _____ and
keep your head _____ to -

240

think of me, and soon I ___ will be there;
geth - er, and call my ___ name out loud;

To bright - en up ___ e -
Soon you'll hear ___ me

- ven your dark - est night. ___
___ knock - in' at ___ your door. ___

You just call ___ out my ___ name,

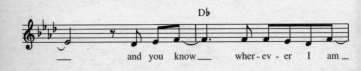

___ and you know ___ wher - ev - er I am ___

___ I'll come run - nin' _____

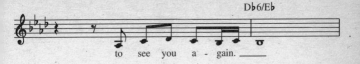
241

to see you a - gain. ____

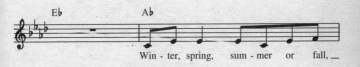
Win - ter, spring, sum - mer or fall, __

all you have to do is call, ___

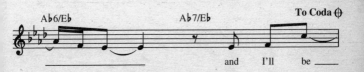
and I'll be ___

To Coda

there. _____ You've Got A Friend..

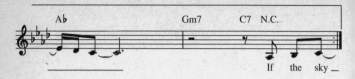

If the sky _

_ there, _ yes, I will. _____ Now

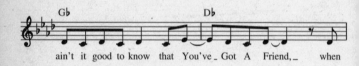

ain't it good to know that You've _ Got A Friend, _ when

peo-ple can be _ so cold. ____ They'll hurt _

_ you, yes, and de-sert _ you, and

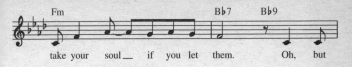

Fm   Bb7   Bb9

take your soul___ if you let them.   Oh, but

Bbm7/Eb   Eb   **D.S. al Coda**

don't you let ___ them.   You just call ___

CODA
Db   Cm7

___ there, ___ yes, I   will. _____

Bbm7 Db6/Eb   Ab   Db/Ab

___ You've Got A Friend. _____   You've Got A

Ab   Db/Ab   **Repeat and Fade**

Friend. ___   Ain't it good ___ to know You've Got A

WILD THING

Words and Music by
CHIP TAYLOR

245

WOOLY BULLY

Words and Music by
DOMINGO SAMUDIO

Moderately

1. Mat - ty told Hat - ty _____ a - bout a
2., 3. *(See additional lyrics)*

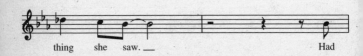

thing she saw. __ Had

two big horns __ and a

wool - ly jaw. __ Wool - y Bul - ly,_____

___ Wool - y Bul - ly,____

Wool - y Bul - ly, ___ Wool - y

Bul - ly, ___ Wool - y Bul - ly. ___

(Instrumental)

Additional Lyrics

2. Hatty told Matty
   Let's don't take no chance
   Let's not be L 7
   Come and learn to dance
   Wooly Bully, Wooly Bully,
   Wooly Bully, Wooly Bully, Wooly Bully.

3. Matty told Hatty
   That's the thing to do,
   Get yo' someone really
   To pull the wool with you -
   Wooly Bully, Wooly Bully,
   Wooly Bully, Wooly Bully, Wooly Bully.

YESTERDAY

Words and Music by JOHN LENNON
and PAUL McCARTNEY

some - thing wrong, now I long for Yes - ter -

day. Yes-ter - day, ____

love was such an eas - y

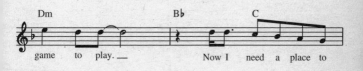

game to play. ____ Now I need a place to

hide a - way, _____ oh

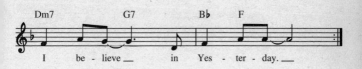

I be - lieve ___ in Yes - ter - day. ___

Mm mm mm mm mm. _____

YOU ARE SO BEAUTIFUL

Words and Music by BILLY PRESTON
and BRUCE FISHER

Moderately slow, expressively

You are so ___ beau-ti-ful ___

to me. You are so ___

___ beau-ti-ful ___ to

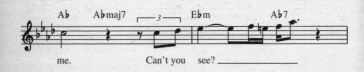

me. Can't you see? _____

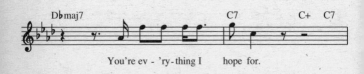

You're ev-'ry-thing I hope for.

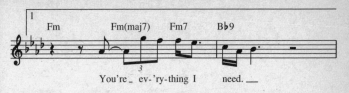

You're ev-'ry-thing I need. ___

You are so ___ beau-ti-ful ___ to

me. _____ You are so ___

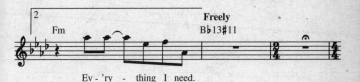

Ev-'ry - thing I need.

Tempo I

You are so ___ beau-ti-ful ___ to ___

___ me. ___

GUITAR CHORD FRAMES

	C	Cm	C+	C6	Cm6
C					

	C#	C#m	C#+	C#6	C#m6
C#/D♭					

	D	Dm	D+	D6	Dm6
D					

	E♭	E♭m	E♭+	E♭6	E♭m6
E♭/D#					

	E	Em	E+	E6	Em6
E					

	F	Fm	F+	F6	Fm6
F					

This guitar chord reference includes 120 commonly used chords. For a more complete guide to guitar chords, see "THE PAPERBACK CHORD BOOK" (HL00702009).

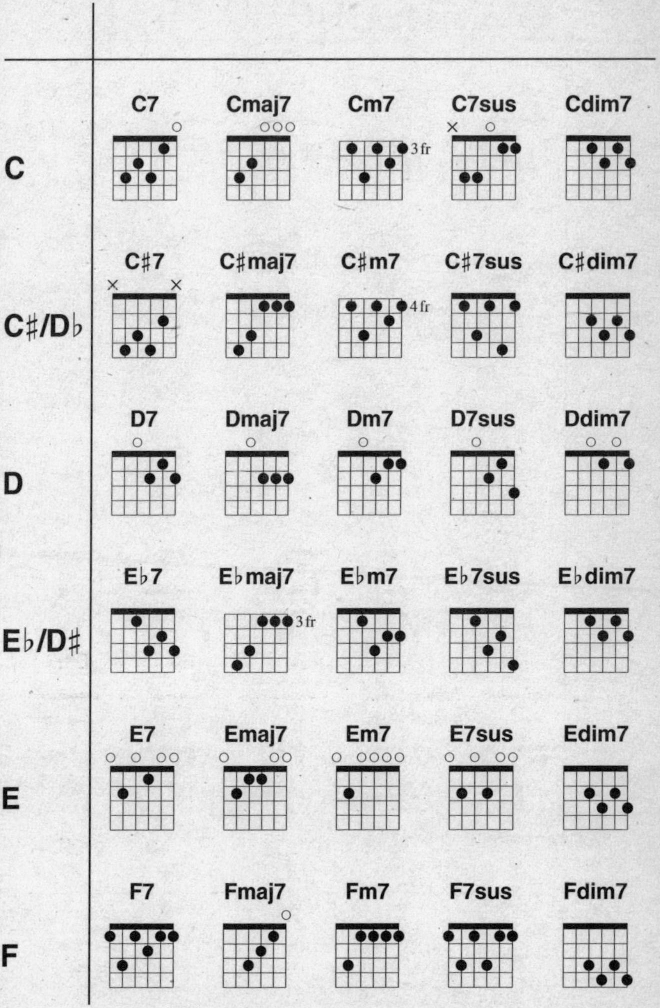
C
C7
Cmaj7
Cm7
3 fr
C7sus
Cdim7
C♯/D♭
C♯7
C♯maj7
C♯m7
4 fr
C♯7sus
C♯dim7
D
D7
Dmaj7
Dm7
D7sus
Ddim7
E♭/D♯
E♭7
E♭maj7
3 fr
E♭m7
E♭7sus
E♭dim7
E
E7
Emaj7
Em7
E7sus
Edim7
F
F7
Fmaj7
Fm7
F7sus
Fdim7

254

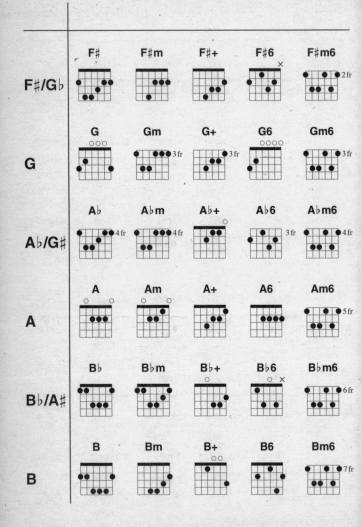

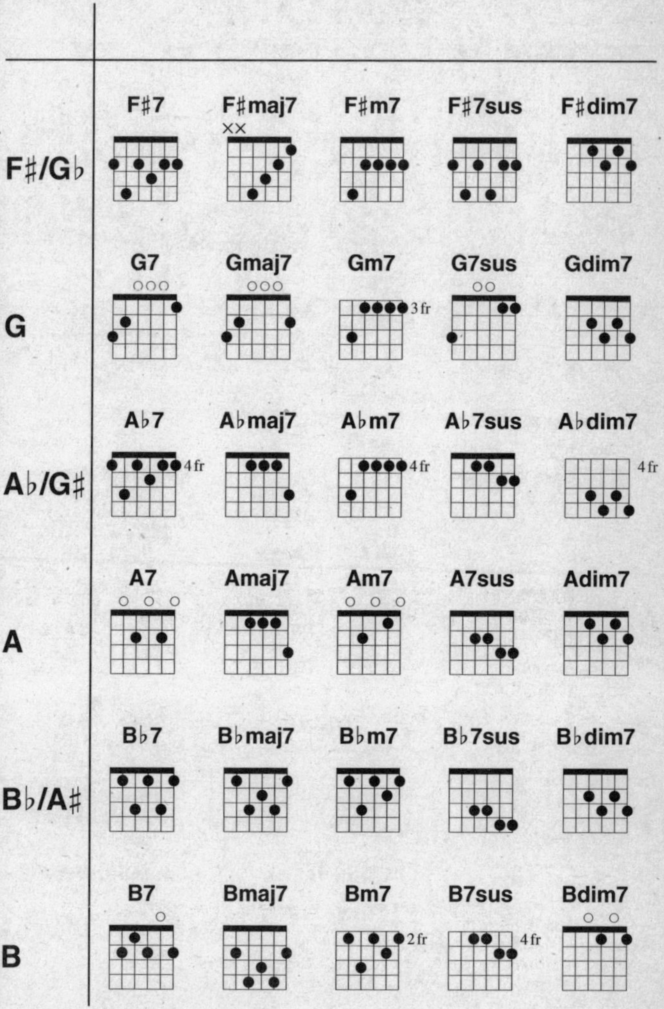
F♯/G♭
F♯7
F♯maj7
F♯m7
F♯7sus
F♯dim7
G
G7
Gmaj7
Gm7
3 fr
G7sus
Gdim7
A♭/G♯
A♭7
4 fr
A♭maj7
A♭m7
4 fr
A♭7sus
A♭dim7
4 fr
A
A7
Amaj7
Am7
A7sus
Adim7
B♭/A♯
B♭7
B♭maj7
B♭m7
B♭7sus
B♭dim7
B
B7
Bmaj7
Bm7
2 fr
B7sus
4 fr
Bdim7